The Brave Journey
from Slavery to Freedom

BY MIIKO SHAFFIER
co-written by Chana Grosser

Illustrated by: Dmitry Gitelman (diemgi.com)
Layout & Design by: Ken Parker (visual-variables.com)

Published by:
Shefer Publishing
www.SheferPublishing.com

For permissions, comments and ordering information write:
Miiko@LearnHebrew.tv

ISBN 978-1-958999-10-3

THE
BRAVE JOURNEY
FROM SLAVERY TO FREEDOM
an EASY EEVREET STORY

BY MIIKO SHAFFIER

SHEFER
———————————
PUBLISHING

Based on Exodus 1:8 to Exodus 2:10
This story can be read like any English story book.
When you get to a Hebrew word, do your best to
sound it out and guess the meaning. You can check the
pronunciation and meaning in the back of the book.

HAVE FUN!

A new and powerful פַּרְעֹה stood looking over מִצְרַיִם. As far as the eye could see there were lush fields and sturdy homes. He saw the beautiful area where the בְּנֵי יִשְׂרָאֵל lived, called GohSHehN, and had a startling realization.

There are so many בְּנֵי יִשְׂרָאֵל, he thought to himself. Before long they might be powerful enough to rebel against me! I need to use their numbers to the advantage of מִצְרַיִם.

"From now on," he commanded in a loud, harsh voice, "בְּנֵי יִשְׂרָאֵל will work for the good of מִצְרַיִם."

At first the בְּנֵי יִשְׂרָאֵל were told to do work in construction jobs and as farmers in the שָׂדֶה.

But despite the harshness of חַיֵּיהֶם, the בְּנֵי יִשְׂרָאֵל were blessed with many strong children. They became an even greater and stronger group in מִצְרַיִם.

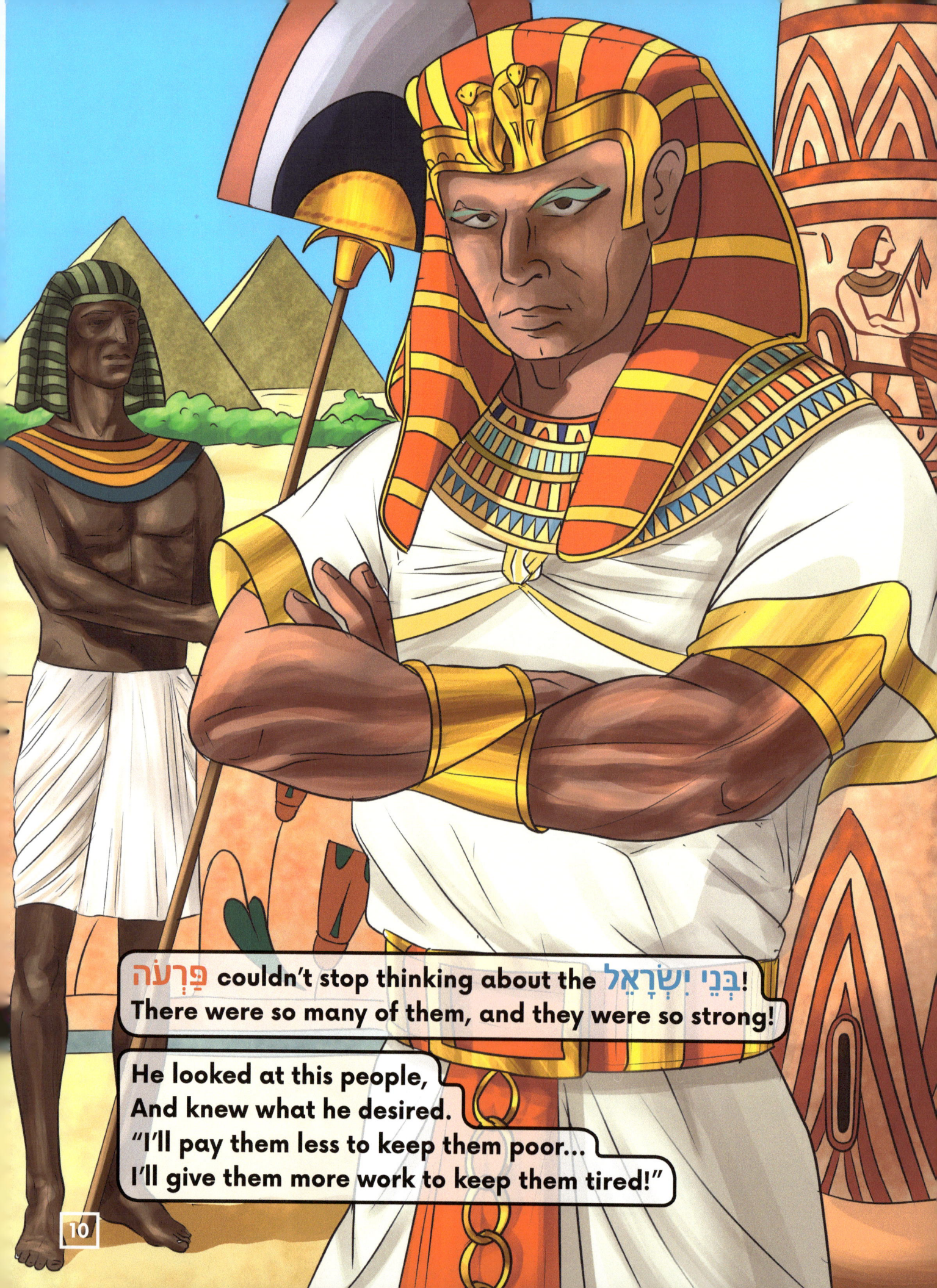

פַּרְעֹה couldn't stop thinking about the בְּנֵי יִשְׂרָאֵל!
There were so many of them, and they were so strong!

He looked at this people,
And knew what he desired.
"I'll pay them less to keep them poor...
I'll give them more work to keep them tired!"

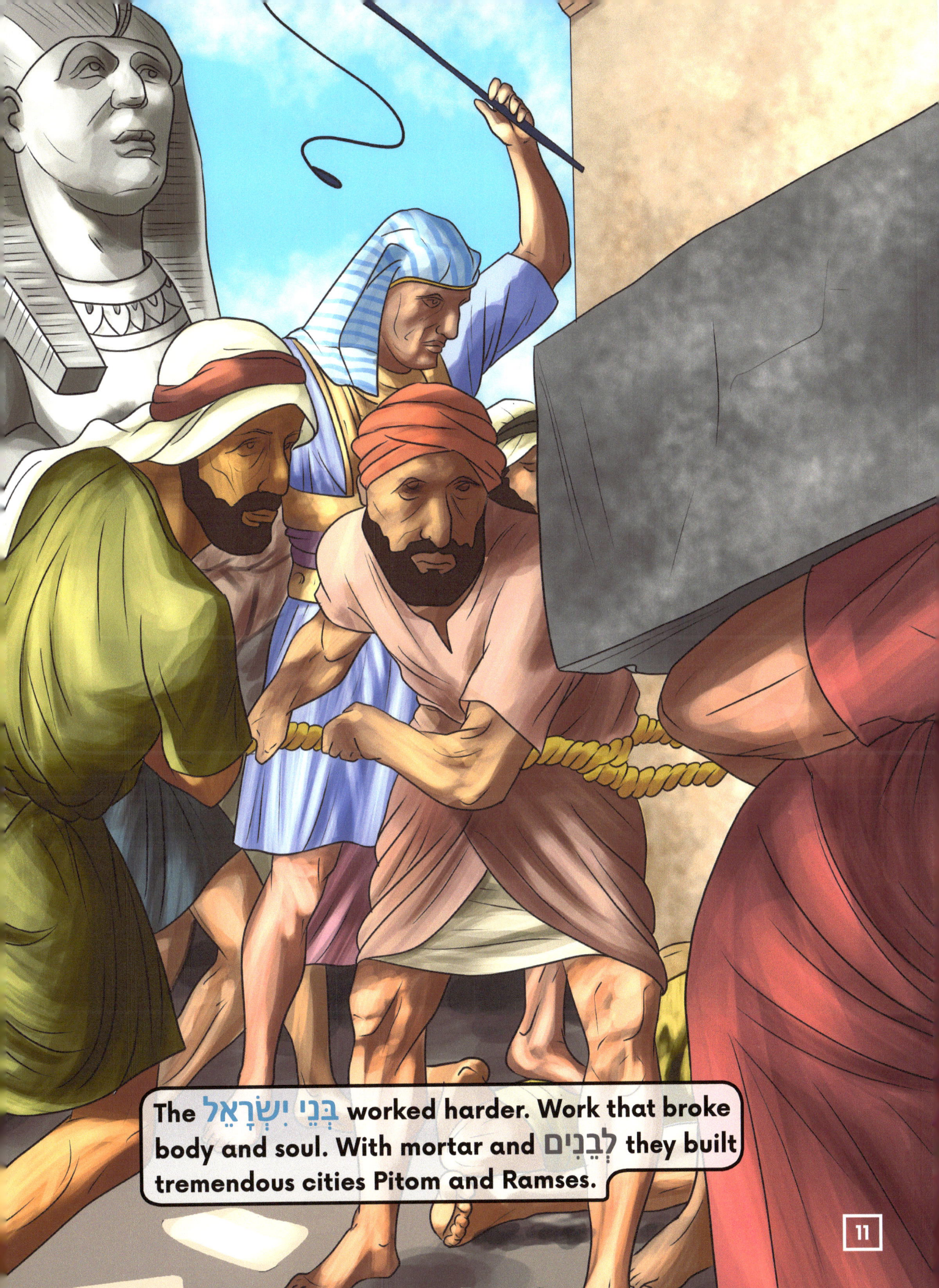

The בְּנֵי יִשְׂרָאֵל worked harder. Work that broke body and soul. With mortar and לְבֵנִים they built tremendous cities Pitom and Ramses.

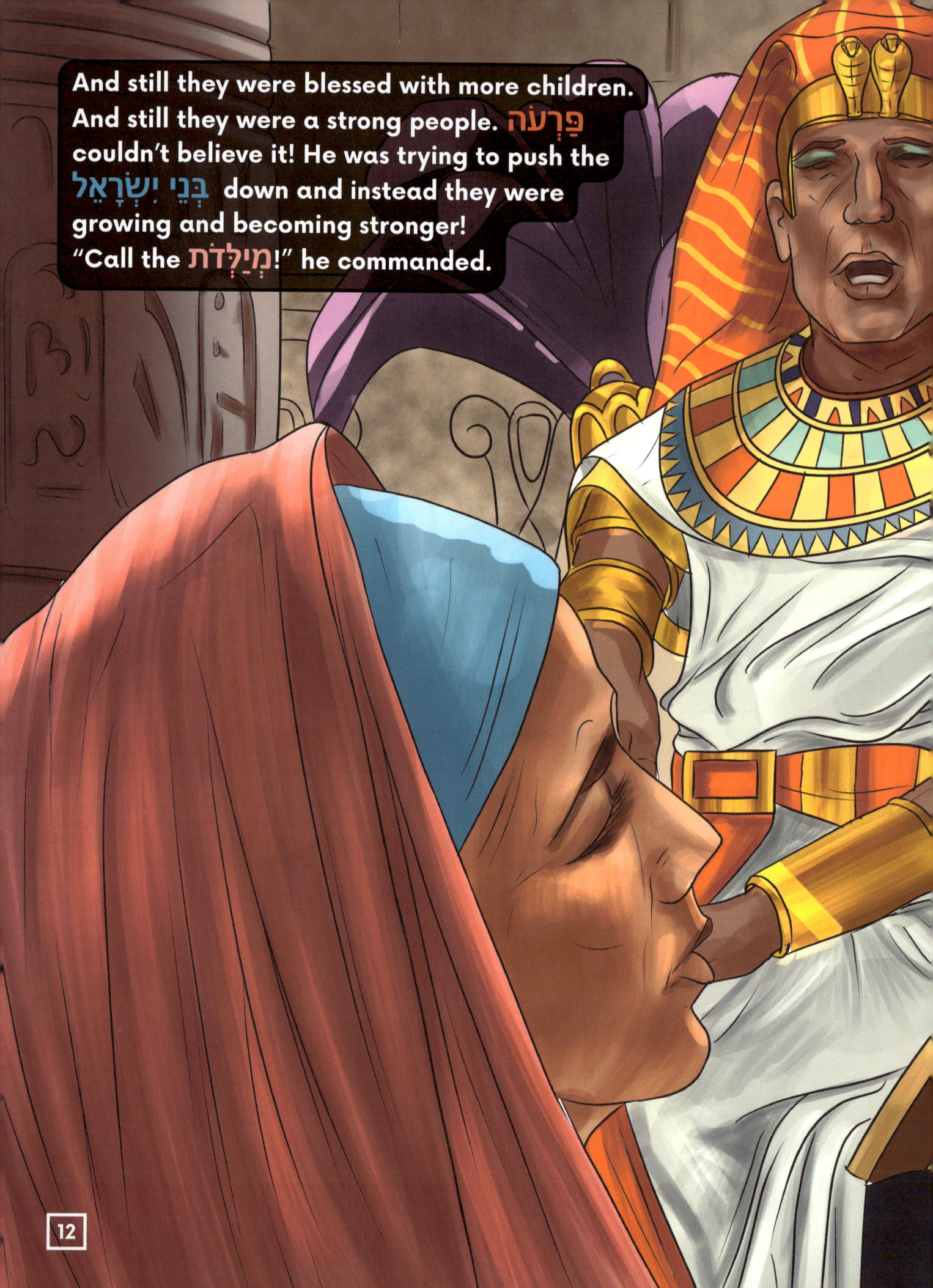

And still they were blessed with more children. And still they were a strong people. פַּרְעֹה couldn't believe it! He was trying to push the בְּנֵי יִשְׂרָאֵל down and instead they were growing and becoming stronger! "Call the מְיַלְדֹת!" he commanded.

SHeeF-RahH and Poo'ahH came right away.
"When you attend the birth of a woman from
בְּנֵי יִשְׂרָאֵל, pay attention." he said.
"If the newborn is a boy, throw him in the Nile."
"If a girl is born, make her חָיָה."

Even though פַּרְעֹה was a terrifying figure in a tremendous palace on a high throne, SHeeF-RahH and Poo'ahH did not obey his command. They knew that G-d is more powerful than any human king! The בְּנֵי יִשְׂרָאֵל continued to increase more and more.

'ahM-RahM and YohCHehVehD were a special couple from the tribe of LehVeeY. They knew that פַּרְעֹה wanted all the baby boys to be thrown into the Nile. But just like SHeeF-RahH and Poo'ahH, they knew that G-d is more powerful than any human king.

One exciting day, 'ahM-RahM and YohCHehVehD had a new baby boy!
Their home was filled with light and joy.
For three long month's YohCHehVehD hid him well.
A family secret no one would tell.

But after three יְרָחִים the baby was too big to hide. How would YohCHehVehD save her sweet baby boy? She thought of a plan and trusted G-d to help her.

YohCHehVehD made a תֵּבַת גֹּמֶא. She lovingly coated it with clay on the inside so it would be smooth, and pitch on the outside so it would be waterproof. It was like a little boat. MeeR-YahM, אֲחֹתוֹ, came to help.

YohCHehVehD put her precious son inside the basket and placed it among the סוף growing along the bank of the Nile River. She told MeeR-YahM "Watch over the basket with your brother. G-d will help!"

G-d makes the sun rise and the flowers grow. He makes the birds sing and the Nile flow. Surely He can save my beautiful brother, she thought.

Through the סוּף, MeeR-YahM heard women's voices! MeeR-YahM's eyes grew larger as she saw BahT-YahH, the daughter of פַּרְעֹה, and her servants appear. They were coming down to the Nile לִרְחֹץ. Would they be the ones to discover her helpless brother?

"What is that heartbreaking sound?" said the daughter of פַּרְעֹה. She discovered it was a baby בֹּכֶה!

Her compassion was greater than her father's order. She decided to save the boy in the basket and raise him in the palace as her own son. She named him "מֹשֶׁה" which means מְשִׁיתִהוּ from the water.

MeeR-YahM was still watching on the bank of the river. She knew this might be her only chance. With a confident voice she called out to the princess. "Would you like me to find a woman to nurse that child?"

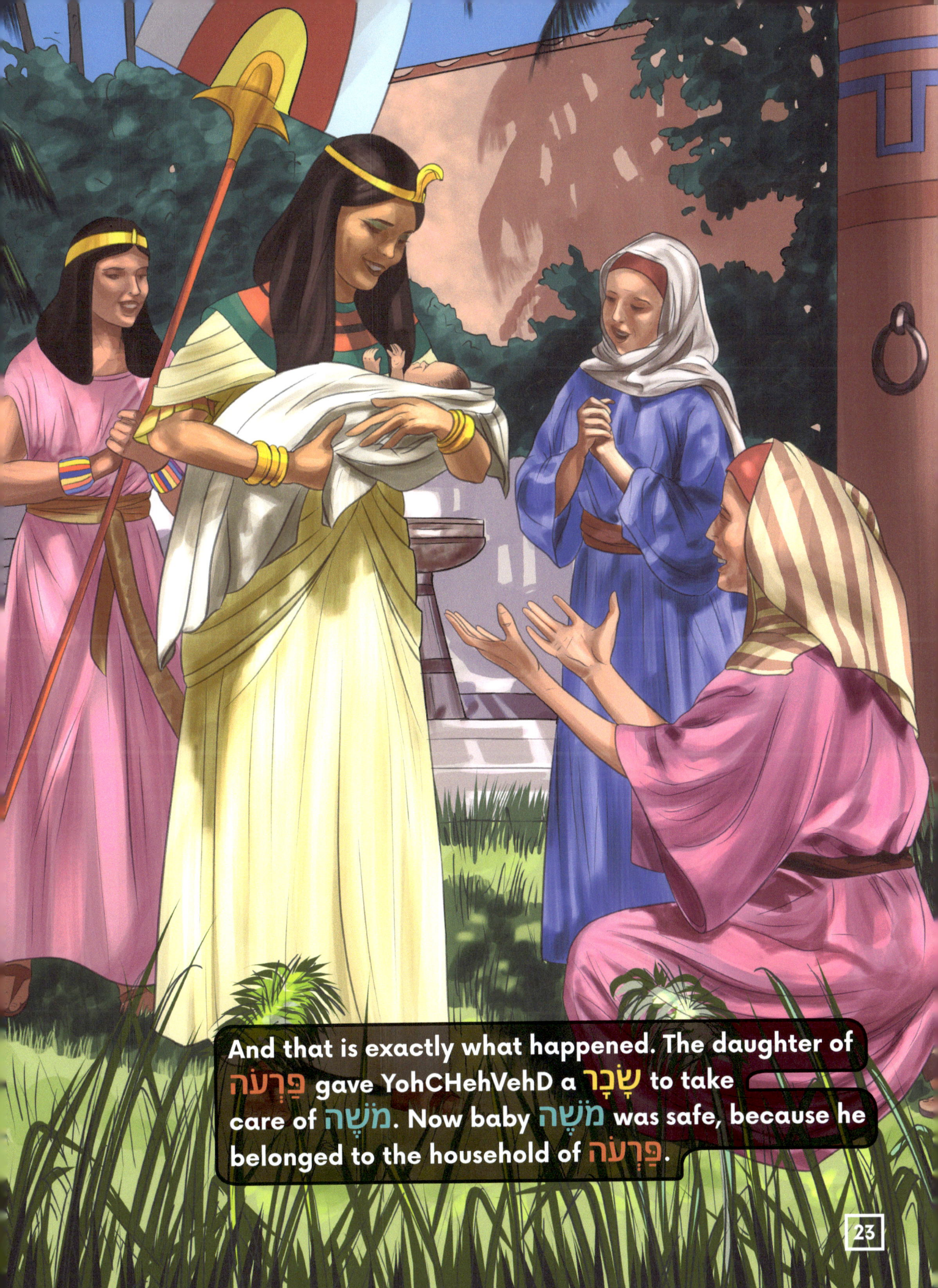

And that is exactly what happened. The daughter of פַּרְעֹה gave YohCHehVehD a שָׂכָר to take care of מֹשֶׁה. Now baby מֹשֶׁה was safe, because he belonged to the household of פַּרְעֹה.

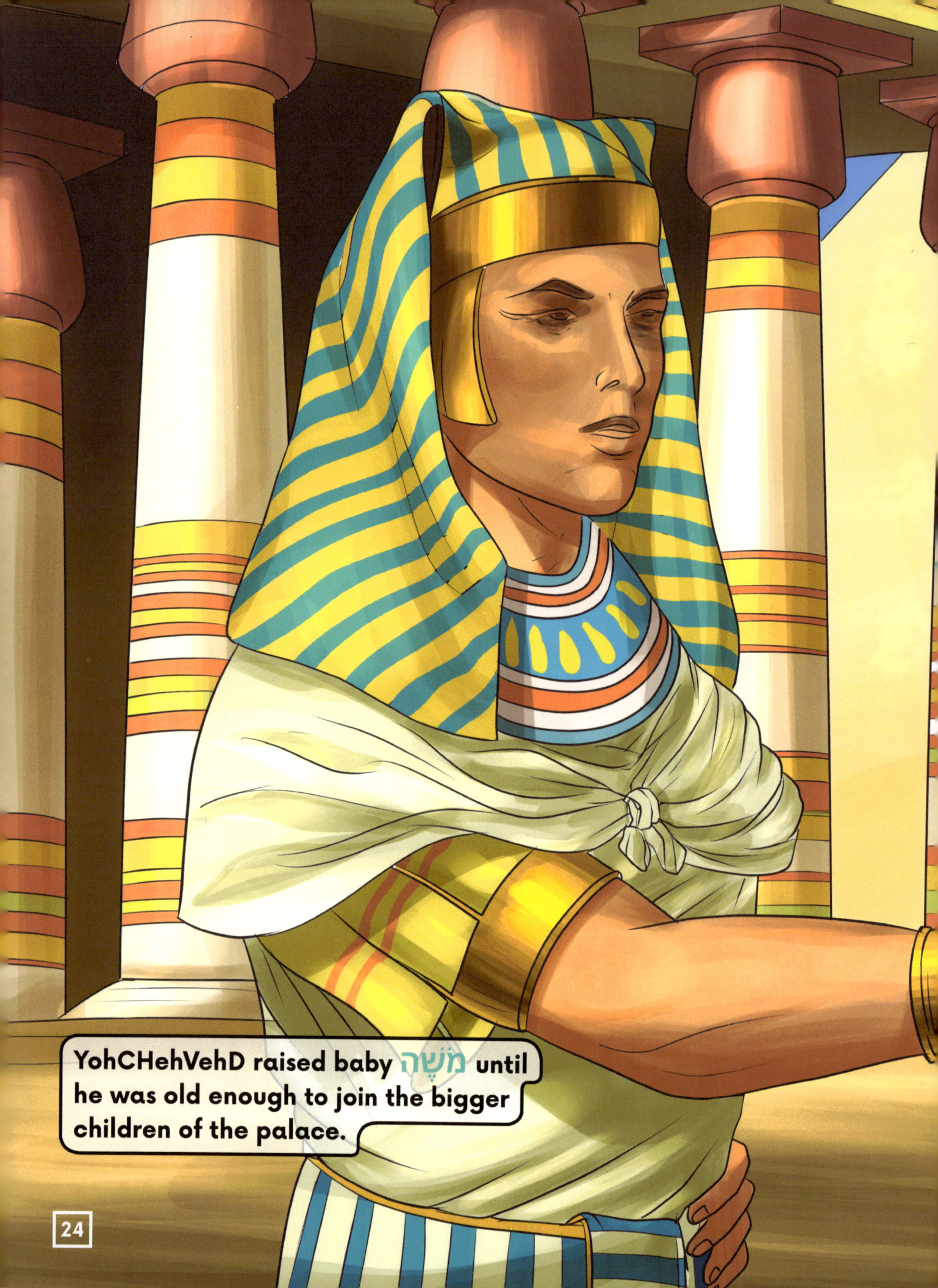

YohCHehVehD raised baby מֹשֶׁה until he was old enough to join the bigger children of the palace.

וַיִּגְדַּל among the children of the palace. He became a regal and educated young man. He learned about royal responsibilities and came to know all the different peoples who lived in מִצְרָיִם.

25

He also knew that he was secretly one of the בְּנֵי יִשְׂרָאֵל.

He knew in his heart that his real brothers were outside, working harder and harder for less and less pay. The בְּנֵי יִשְׂרָאֵל had become slaves to the Egyptians and were whipped and beaten.

He was so different from his suffering brothers.

One day soon, with faith in the one true G-d, מֹשֶׁה would rejoin his people. His sister MeeR-YahM who watched over him as a baby in the Nile would be by his side. His brother 'ahHahRohN would join him too. Together, with great miracles from G-d, they would confront the powerful פַּרְעֹה and lead the בְּנֵי יִשְׂרָאֵל away from the slavery of מִצְרַיִם.

Here are the Hebrew words from this *Easy Eevreet Story*:

 פַּרְעֹה   PahR-'ohH - **EGYPTIAN KING/PHAROAH** | p. 6,10,12,14,15,20, 23,24,28

 מִצְרָיִם   MeeTZ-RahYeeM - **EGYPT** | p. 6,7,9,25,28

 בְּנֵי יִשְׂרָאֵל   B-NehY YeeS-Rah'ehL | p. 6,7-14,26,27,28

B-NehY means children and YeeS-Rah'ehL means Israel.
Together that means **CHILDREN OF ISRAEL** or **ISRAELITE.**

 שָׂדֶה   SahDehH - **FIELD** | p. 8

חַיֵּיהֶם   CHahYehYHehM - **(THEIR) LIVES** | p. 9

לְבֵנִים   L-VehNeeYM - **BRICKS** | p. 11

מְיַלְדֹת   M-YahL-DohT - **MIDWIVES** | p. 12

חָיָה   CHahYahH - **LIVE (FEMININE)** | p. 13

For a boy use the word חַי CHahY.

 יְרָחִים   Y-RahCHeeYM - **MOONS** | p. 16

If you want to say moon use the word
יֶרַח YahRehahCH.

 תֵּבַת גֹּמֶא

TehVahT GohMeh' - **WICKER BASKET** | p. 16

(literally wicker box or wicker container)

אֲחֹתוֹ

'ahCHohToh - **HIS SISTER** | p. 16

סוּף

SooF - **REEDS** | p. 17,20

You may have heard of the Red Sea. In the Bible it's called: יַם סוּף YahM SooF - **SEA OF REEDS**
At some point someone made a mistake when they were translating and the Sea of Reeds became known as the Red Sea. I'll tell you, it's not red but it does have many reeds.

רָחֹק

RahCHohK - **FAR** | p. 18

לִרְחֹץ

LeeR-CHohTZ - **TO WASH/TO BATHE** | p. 20

Here are some other ways you might use this word:

רָחַצְתִּי

RahCHahTZ-TeeY - **(I) WASHED**

רָחַץ

RahCHahTZ - **(HE) WASHED**

רָחַצְתָּ

RahCHahTZ-Tah - **(YOU) WASHED**

רָחֲצוּ

RahCHahTZoo - **(THEY) WASHED**

You did it! You're learning Hebrew! And you learned some interesting facts along the way. Try asking people if they know the real name of the Red Sea. Or if they can tell you how Moses got his name. I bet you'll surprise them with the answers.

Hi!

My name is **Miiko.** I live in Be'er Sheva, Israel. My husband Aaron and I have nine kids: Menucha, Mendel, Dovi, Yisroel, Freida, Devora, Fitche, Geula, and Azaria.

I teach Hebrew reading with a fun little book called *Learn to Read Hebrew in 6 Weeks!*

My second book *The Hebrew Workbook* teaches readers to write in Hebrew.

The Brave Journey from Slavery to Freedom is part of a series of storybooks that teach Hebrew vocabulary to kids.

I'm so pleased to be a part of your Hebrew journey. If you have any questions or want to say hi please send me an email! **Miiko@LearnHebrew.tv**

To the Parents

This book is designed to teach Hebrew vocabulary to people who already know how to read the Hebrew alphabet. While reading this Bible story in English you'll come across Hebrew words embedded in the text. Sound out the words and try to guess their meaning from the context. Check the key in the back of the book to see if you were right.

I've chosen to transliterate the names of the biblical characters mentioned in this story so that you'll learn the authentic Hebrew pronunciation of these biblical names.

Transliteration

The Brave Journey from Slavery to Freedom uses the same system of transliteration as my first book *Learn to Read Hebrew in 6 Weeks!*

I came up with a unique transliteration system. It's designed to have the reader pronouncing the Hebrew words accurately without ever having heard a Hebrew speaker pronounce those words.

Here's a breakdown of the system:

Each consonant is represented as a capital letter and each vowel by small letters.

The silent letters 'ahLehF (א) and 'ahYeeN (ע) are represented by an apostrophe (')

The silent vowel 'Sh-Vah' (:) is represented as a hyphen (-).

An important exception to make note of:
The CH does not represent the ch sound like in *chair* or *chest*. In fact, Hebrew doesn't have the ch sound like *chair* or *chest* at all.

The CH represents the letters CHehT(ח) and CHahF(כ) and Final ChahF(ך). These letters make a sound not found in the English language. It's a chokey sound that almost sounds like a kitten purring but much harsher. Think about the name of the composer Bach. From what my Spanish speaking students tell me, it's the same sound as the guttural J in Spanish.

Let's look at the first word in the Hebrew Scripture as an example of how my system works:

בְּרֵאשִׁית

I transliterate it:
B-Reh'SHeeYT

Others may transliterate Bereshit or Bresheet but then you wouldn't know if the vowels are long or short.

If you learned to read Hebrew using my other book, you are already well familiar with this system. But in case you learned to read Hebrew elsewhere, here's a key to make sure it's clear.

א	ב	ב	ג	ד	ה	ו
'	B	V	G	D	H	V

ז	ח	ט	י	כּ	כ	ך
Z	CH	T	Y	K	CH	CH

ל	מ	ם	נ	ן	ס	ע
L	M	M	N	N	S	'

פ	ף	פ	צ	ץ	ק	ר
P	F	F	TZ	TZ	K	R

שׁ	תּ	ת
SH	T	T

דַ	ֶ	וֹ	וּ	ִ	ְ
ah	eh	oo	oh	ee	-

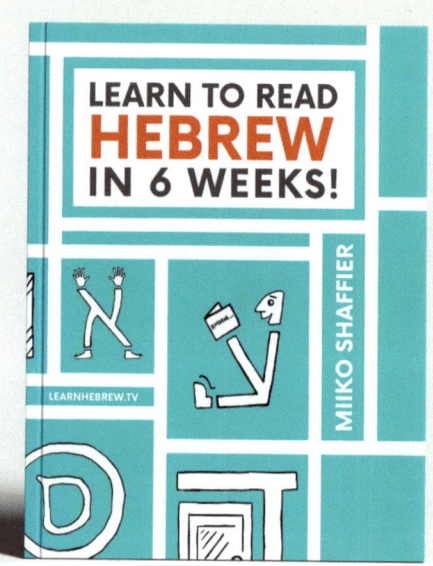